Proverbs
for the Family

BY

LYNDA SAVAGE, M.S.

First Edition
© 2002 Lynda Savage

ISBN 1-886028-55-9

Library of Congress Catalog Card Number: 2002-2090989

Savage
PRESS

Published by: Savage Press
P.O. Box 115
Superior, WI 54880
715/394-9513

E-mail: mail@savpress.com
Web Site: www.savpress.com

Printed in the U.S.A.

Acknowledgments

I am indebted to the myriad of people who have shared their hearts with me in therapy. Their search for a better way connects me to my own family's search for a better way. I deeply respect the people at the Center for Family Healing. They have been a great blessing to me. I would like to thank Brenda Spina, M.S. for her faithful friendship and support. I would also like to thank my brother Mike, for his expertise and encouragement. Without the depth of connection that all of these people have been willing to share, this book would not exist.

Lynda Savage

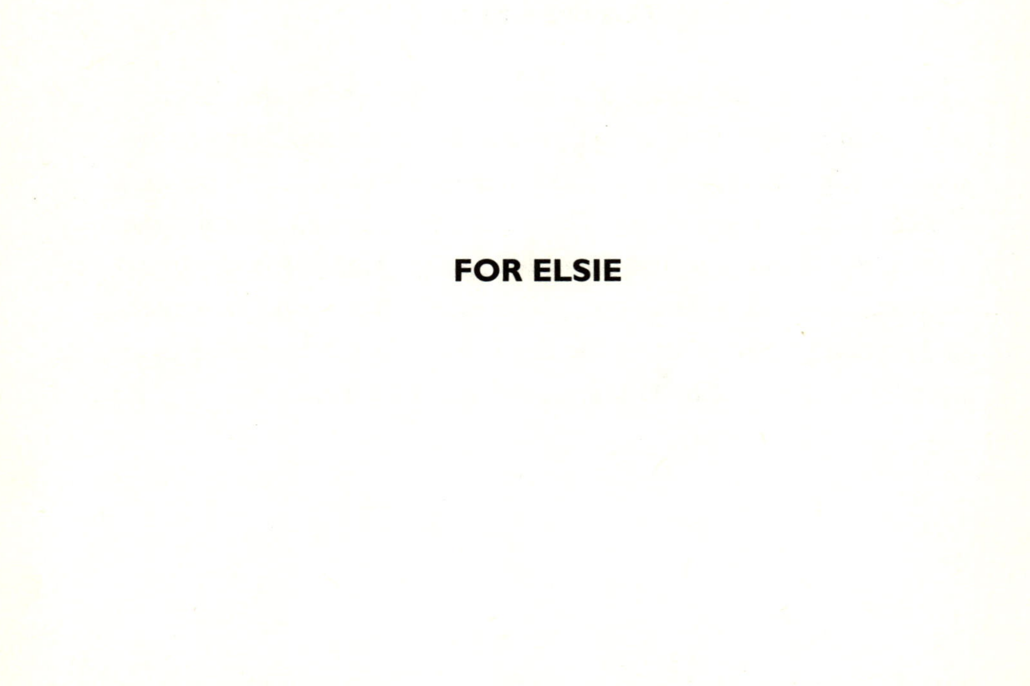
FOR ELSIE

APPROACHING THIS BOOK

Proverbs for the Family is meant to evoke a response from the reader. Some responses may be: "aha," some "that can't be true." Whatever your reaction, the value to the reader is to consider these Proverbs in light of a desire to improve important relationships. As you weigh the truth of each statement, you will increase your ability to give understanding and support to others. Read first the individual Proverbs. Come to your own resonance or dissonance with these nuggets of information. Consider referring to the comments in the back of the book after you have a sense of your own ideas about what is being said. Then "compare and contrast" your ideas with the author.

Lynda

A covenant before God cannot effectively be broken by man.

*C*hildren never get over divorce.

3

A child's voice is not heard by depressed adults.

4

*I*f you care to and maybe dare to observe, a child involved with you will show you uncomfortable sides of your nature.

5

*T*hat "some day," when there will only be calmness, peace, and no worries, is not going to come.

*W*aiting for your spouse or child to grow up keeps you from the richness of engaging them now.

*I*n communication, waiting for God's timing has great reward.

People need to know they belong.

9

*A*rbitrarily taking away of a sense of belonging by any family member, by another, will be punished in some way.

10

*W*ives who speak of their husband's strengths are upheld.

A sudden or discovered resonance with someone outside of your marital commitment can be interpreted as biological, not spiritual; it can be resisted.

12

*I*nviting Jesus in to how you really feel about any addiction, at any level, at any time, brings a Beloved Friend alongside you to stop the self-destruction.

13

Young children, if they cannot be comforted, are not purposefully against you.

*A*dolescents do not lay awake at night trying to think of ways to make your life miserable.

*C*hildren raising each other are tyrants.

If a child is in a coalition with one parent against the other parent, it is not the fault of the child.

Distant fathers give up their position until they return to the family in truth.

18

*D*istant parents allow for stray affections in their children.

Loss not grieved keeps families stuck.

20

*F*or family members to grow in responsibility, the heat needs to stay where it belongs.

*S*haming behaviors and person-to-person attempts at annihilation are relatives.

Shaming: Put-down, haughty look, attitude of "you are nothing," "you need not exist," attitude of "you are very faulty," "something is very wrong with you."

*F*amily members who do
not challenge do not love.

*A*nother chance, breathes life into families.

*A*nother chance, breathes life into relationships.

25

*O*ffenses faced without shaming build a rock solid foundation.

*M*en who flee create women who fear.

Gender interchangeable

*W*omen who constantly pursue create fleeing men.

Gender interchangeable

*H*usbands who husband
a wife live in a garden.

Correction is a reward.

*C*orrection is a gift.

31

A dirty look meant to shame, God hates.

*P*eople in the upper parts of family hierarchy are unaware of their power over the people in the lower parts.

33

*U*sing people in the
lower parts of your family
hierarchy is cowardice.

34

The habit of cutting off emotional connection for the purpose of punishment will not produce control; it will produce loneliness and bitterness.

The habit of nagging about faults or analyzing another's shortcomings for sport produces bitterness and lack of growth.

God is real, the Bible is Truth, Jesus lives and the Holy Spirit is available.

*F*orgiveness is the essence of God, relationship and peace.

38

*T*o pursue forgiveness is to pursue love.

*N*ot accepting how you feel or not wanting to know how you feel, can become practiced dishonesty.

40

*W*anting the best for others without thought for oneself can be a way of hiding.

*M*others or Fathers without support can become driven and childlike at the same time.

42

*F*athers can hide behind production and never know they are needed as people.

43

*T*eens who become parents are in danger of raising old people in young bodies.

44

*Youth is a matter of joy,
not age.*

45

Be aware that if you recruit a child to help you parent, you have "spoused" the child.

*I*f you have "spoused" a child, make every effort to let the child play.

47

*I*f you have a "spoused" child, do not be jealous if the child finds a substitute parent who will allow childlike behavior.

*I*t takes great effort and exceeding grace from God for a single parent in spirit or in fact, not to "spouse" a child.

Another word for a "spoused" child is a parentified child.

49

A parentified child will need help to fill the empty spaces as an adult.

A parentified child may be easily used when an adult.

51

A parentified child may easily hide behind emotional, physical and spiritual work as an adult.

*I*t's important to see your friends as relationship, not opportunity.

53

*E*ach child's perspective,
when shared with sincerity,
is to be honored.

54

*N*o matter the age of a person in a family, each is equal in worth and dignity.

55

Promoting the family as a team, working at ways to make the family operate better as a whole...is better than fostering competition within.

We are different and we are the same. We come close and we go away.

57

*T*o keep your loved ones at a distance because you fear loss, causes loss.

58

Give your children
the blessing to be more
successful than you.

*L*et your children grieve.

*L*et yourself grieve.

*D*o not enlist your children to be your main source of emotional support.

*A*dults who try to accomplish the impossible sometimes have a father or mother who failed at something important.

63

When you speak to your child about his or her behavior, do not ask, "Why did you do this or that?" They will say, "I don't know" or "because." Say, "Because you did this or that, this consequence will happen."

*C*hildren need directness,
not questions.

65

*I*t's unfair to ask a question about your child's behavior when you already know the answer.

*U*se praise sparingly. It emphasizes what you think.

67

Give encouragement more than praise. Praise focuses on the giver of the words, encouragement on the efforts of the recipient of the words.

*D*escriptive praise goes farther and gives more care than a simple praise statement.

*W*hen you have a point
of disagreement, review
what is going on with you
about the issue ten times
more than you dwell on the
other person's fault.

70

Anger is a way of connecting. Maybe not the best way, but still a way.

*G*od knows all about your spouse and you. Do what it takes to hear what God wants to tell you about your spouse and your marriage.

72

*I*f you believe your spouse is no better and no worse than you, this belief will result in fair play.

*P*eople's ideas of themselves are extremely influenced by how their spouse sees them.

*I*t's a good rule that each family member gets to start new every morning without recrimination.

*I*nvite Jesus in to exactly how you feel or think about a thing.

PROVERBS, COMMENTS and RESOURCES

1. A covenant before God...

Comment: God's word to man cannot be broken. He is not a man that he should lie (Numbers 23:19).

Suggested Reading: Derek Prince, *The Marriage Covenant* (New Kensington, PA: Whittaker House Publishers, 1978).

2. Children never...

Comment: For children there is no "getting over" parents divorcing. It is worse than death because no one is actually dead. As long as the children are alive, their parents' union is a living thing though inextricably changed for all time in a way that disturbs the child's trust forever.

Suggested Reading: Judith Wallerstein & Sandra Blakeslee, *Second Chances* (New York: Ticknor & Fields, 1989).

3. A child's voice...

Comment: Depression by its nature is a dulling of the ability to be sensitive to others. A caregiver may have little to give in a depressed state. Therefore, it is important for a depressed caregiver to address depression, if not for themselves, for those who depend on them.

4. If you care to observe...

Comment: Children do and say what they see and hear. You will see yourself in them, both the good and the bad, if you care and maybe dare, to look.

5. That "some day"...

Comment: People wait to live. They wait for the day when everything is as it is "supposed to be." The time you had perhaps hoped for when all will be totally well with every aspect of your being, does not happen in an imperfect world where we are growing, changing, interacting with others and growing older. Peace in the Lord exists, however, even when things are imperfect.

6. Waiting for your spouse or child...

Comment: People sometime put off accepting a mate, friend or child. They are waiting for a time when the other person is more acceptable. Before allowing them in emotionally to a place of care, concern and acceptance, people want others to change, grow-up, or develop this or that. The change you are waiting for may never happen because of the very fact that you are not accepting.

7. In communication...

Comment: When we have an answer to someone's question, spoken or unspoken, we sometimes rush in human excitement to answer, validate, tell or provide before we check in with God's timing on the thing or even if we should give the help at all. If God has given you some answers, ask for the wisdom you need in how and if to apply these answers.

8. People need...

Comment: Belonging and attachment are essential for growth. Those who do not belong or do not feel attached wither and die.

"During the 19th century more than half of the infants died in their first year of life from a disease called marasmus, a Greek word meaning "wasting away." As late as the 1920's according to Montagu, the death rate for infants under one year of age in various U.S. foundling institutions was close to 100%! Dr. Henry Chapin's detective work on this alarming phenomenon is a fascinating tale.

"A distinguished New York pediatrician, Dr. Chapin noted that the infants were kept in sterile, neat, tidy wards, but were rarely picked up. Chapin brought in women to hold the babies, coo to them, and stroke them, and the mortality rate dropped dramatically." Alan McGinnis, *The Friendship Factor* (Minneapolis, MN: Augsburg Publishing House, 1979, p. 86).

Suggested Reading: John Bowlby, *Attachment and Loss* (New York: Basic Books, Inc., 1980).

9. Arbitrary taking away of...

Comment: If people get involved in the type of conflict that is common in families wherein one person suggests, intimates or actually makes movement which is meant to take away another's sense of belonging, the other family member or loved one will most likely respond by trying to do the same back.

10. Wives who...

Suggested Reading: "An excellent wife is the crown of her husband..." (Proverbs 12:4).

11. A sudden or discovered reso-nance with someone outside of your marital commitment...

Comment: A certain resonance, even an evocative emotional response, needs to be treated as something needing cognitive distance. In order to make good decisions about what the sudden resonance means and what needs to be done about the sudden resonance, a distance from the person is required. A sudden resonance can be resisted, and must be resisted, potentially over and over again. These sudden resonances can be very strong. We have a template of experience within ourselves. There are people who "ring the bell" of that template. You have choices regarding this.

12. Inviting Jesus in...

Comment: Inviting Jesus in to how you really feel requires that you take time to come before Him. This taking time to come before Him can be as you're driving or walking or even in the most mundane of experiences. It means to turn your attention to Jesus and, for example, say to Him, "look what's happening, look how I'm feeling, you can see what's going on with me, I invite You in to this. Be with me in it. Please feel this with me and guide me through it."

13. Young children...

Comment: So often, tired parents come to believe that if children are not responding to their efforts at comforting a child in distress, somehow a connection is made that the child is rejecting the parent. This is untrue. And, though it may never be known what the trouble is with a child, you can one hundred percent be assured that the child is not rejecting you personally if they are not able to be comforted. Young children's minds and motives do not operate the way adult minds operate. Sometimes it's a good idea to put this truth on the refrigerator or somewhere where you can be reminded of this.

14. Adolescents do not...

Comment: Adolescents want firm boundaries. They are also intensely involved with self. Making you miserable is rarely at the forefront of their minds. Many, if abused consistently, may want to hurt parents, but for the most part, adolescents want to know who they are and how they fit into the scheme of possibilities for their life rather than focusing on revenge.

15. Children raising each other...

Comment: A child is a child. They do not have the wherewithall to do a parent's job. Where they have to "go" emotionally to enforce boundaries with other children, is a tyrannical place. (This is also true for parents who act as children do.)

16. If a child is in a coalition...

Comment: Very subtly parents recruit children to be in a type of special understanding, often against the other parent. Small, intimate sharings about the inadequacies of the other parent or even supposedly "funny" comments regarding the other parent to the child creates a coalition that you, the parent, may not like or you may not want to deal with in future years. When the child, no matter how old, sees that they were emotionally recruited for your protection and not for theirs, they will feel tricked.

17. Distant fathers...

Comment: Fathers sometimes fool themselves by thinking that they are away making money or involved in some important project which justifies them leaving the fathering and mothering to the mother. Children may be disrespectful and or distant strangers to the father in cases such as this. When fathers return and truly connect with their children or make efforts to connect (which is almost as good as actually connecting) children eventually tend to recognize and begin to give respect to the father who has been distant. By connection, I mean an honest effort to really give and receive personal attention and care.

18. Distant parents...

Comment: Children will try to get their needs met with other people, such as teachers, neighbors or friends, if parents are not providing the type of nurturance that is needed.

19. Loss not grieved...

Comment: If grief is avoided, it is like not noticing you are in a swamp with your feet in six inches of mud and are unable to move.

20. For family members to grow...

Comment: For maturation and age appropriate growing, responsibilities need to be in appropriate places in families. Parents need to be parents, children and all members need to be responsible for actions at age appropriate levels.

21. Shaming...

Comment: Shaming is a type of put-down that suggests that the other person should not live. The shaming individual is more or less stating to the other individual that something is so wrong with them that they should not have a place on the planet. Shaming in the emotional sense is very close to murder, at least in attitude.

22. Family members who do not challenge...

Comment: Challenge is a gift most of the time. Challenges worked through, create trust. Challenges ignored create more challenges.

23. Another chance...families.

Comment: A good rule for a family or for a work environment is that every morning there is a new chance with all concerned. In other words, forgiveness is the theme of each new day. With this standard in mind, health is more likely in families or in groups.

24. Another chance...relationships.

Comment: Commit to a rule in your relationships that with a new day comes forgiveness and a fresh start.

25. Offenses faced without shaming...

Comment: Developing rules that include talking about differences without put-downs, build strong foundations for any relationship. "A soft answer turns away wrath, but a harsh word stirs up anger." (Proverbs 15:1).

26. Men who flee...

Comment: Though it is not specific to the male gender, abandonment in a committed relationship by a man will create a woman who is insecure and fearful.

27. Women who constantly pursue...

Comment: A continual seeker of involvement will create an atmosphere wherein the pursued will want distance.

28. Husbands who husband a wife...

Comment: One definition of a husband is an expert in nourishment and growth.

29. Correction is...reward.

Comment: When a person can receive correction, their life grows in quality, which in itself is rewarding.

Suggested Reading: The Book of Proverbs.

30. Correction is...gift.

Comment: Correction, if you are able to hear it, may be seen as a gift.

31. A dirty look...

Comment: A dirty look or a haughty look makes for a communication which indicates that the person receiving the look is not worthy to exist on the same planet or that there is something deeply wrong with that individual in the depth of their being. This is exactly opposite from what God desires to communicate, which is that He loves each person. (Proverbs 8:13; Proverbs 6:13-19).

32. People in the upper parts of the family hierarchy...

Comment: Parents, bosses, teachers; all have great impact on those "under" them. They are often not aware of their impact on those "under" them.

33. Using people...

Comment: Cowardice is hiding. Very often a person who is using other people is not risking the mental work or emotional work involvement that they need to be risking for the betterment of the family.

34. The habit of cutting off emotional connection...

Comment: Emotional cut-off is generally just plain wrong.

39. Not accepting how you feel...practiced dishonesty.

Comment: If you continue to ignore the feelings God gave you (this doesn't mean your behavior is dictated by your feelings), you may not have enough information to be honest.

40. Wanting the best for others...

Comment: People can hide in service to others.

A person in this position needs to serve only as God leads. They need to ask God to help them by discerning what is appropriate service and what is hiding through over-activity.

41. Mothers or fathers without support...

Comment: It is easy for parents to become worn out. The emotional output of a mother with young children, for example, has been likened to the energy output an astronaut exerts preparing for a spacewalk. A parent without emotional/spiritual support can become drained like a battery without a generator.

42. Fathers can hide behind production...

Comment: Some fathers have not been trained to see the delight in their spouse or children when they walk into a room. They are unaware of their value as a loved part of the family.

43. Teens who become parents...

Comment: The teen who becomes a parent tends to place a lot of responsibility on their children. Children who are raised with overwhelming responsibility become old before their time.

45. Be aware...you have "spoused"...

Comment: This means you have asked the child to become a provider of adult tasks and emotions—even adults have difficulties with parenting so to ask a child for these things is intensely unfair. I sometimes cringe when I hear parents continually remarking about what

a great help so & so child is with the younger children. I wonder if that child is seen as a child by the parents.

46. If you have "spoused"...

Comment: When children are overly or covertly "asked" to take on emotional, physical or spiritual responsibilities that an adult should be taking in that family unit, the child needs to be recognized as a child, not a utilitarian person who gives themselves up for the family.

47. If you have "spoused"... childlike behavior

Comment: Children who have been "spoused," may find a place or a person who sees them as a child. Children need to be children.

48. It takes...single parent...

Comment: Single parents have a very difficult task. Children shoulder more than single parents may be aware of.

49. A parentified...fill the gaps...

Comment: Often an overly responsible child (they may not have that appearance) will have unfinished developmental stages to make whole as an adult. God is an expert at this.

50. A parentified...may be easily used...

Comment: Parentified children have been trained to live to please others in positions above them. Without understanding this dynamic as an adult, they may continue the pattern of living nearly entirely for others' approval.

51. A parentified child may easily hide...as an adult.

Comment: A parentified child knows how to work in a number of ways that our society applauds. The emptiness of the missing gaps from childhood can be hidden by emotional, physical or spiritual work as an adult.

52. It's important to...relationships, not opportunity.

Comment: If you are someone who has a job to do, needs help, or wants to make money, be aware that it is a temptation to do it the easy way and use vulnerable people to accomplish your tasks rather than more appropriate sources.

53. Each child's perspective...

Comment: Never laugh at, scorn, or ignore a child's contribution to the situation when the offering is sincere.

54. No matter the age of a person...

Comment: Check yourself on this. Do you really believe each person in the family is equal before the Lord and equal in worth? If you don't really believe this, you will be resented and you will teach others to resent each other in the family.

55. Promoting the family as a team...

Comment: The challenge of parents, or we can say the executives of a family, is to keep the focus of family members on how satisfying it is for each one in the family at each age and stage, to make things work together so everyone benefits. If this is not consistently done, who is "good" and who is "bad" will continually be the topic for parents to make "judgments" about. Better a coach/player than a judge.

56. We are different and...

Comment: Relationships and people are like seasons. The same piece of land experiences the earth's changes, but it continues to be the same piece of land.

57. To keep your loved one...

Comment: Unconscious distancing of a loved one, for example, a child, because one of your other children has perhaps died, will compound loss. Ask God to help you with any unfinished grieving so solid connections with your loved ones can take place.

58. Give your children the blessing...

Comment: Check yourself to see whether or not you have entitled your children to be more successful than you.

59. & 60. Let your children/yourself grieve.

Comment: It feels awkward perhaps to have mad, sad, bad feelings. It is important to allow for these feelings to go through the stages of grief.

61. Do not enlist...

Comment: It is important to gain your main sources of emotional support from people at the same level of age and stage development as you.

64. Adults who try...

Comment: Trying to do the impossible is a set-up for failure and may repeat the "failure" of the parent(s).

67. Descriptive praise...

Comment: Descriptive praise combines a good comment about what you think: "That's great," along with a description of why you think it is "great." For example: "Because you took time to be careful."

68. Give encouragement...

Comment: Encouragement always focuses on the effort of the other. For example: "You worked hard on that and you seem to have a lot of satisfaction with it."

70. Anger is...

Comment: This may not be the way of effectiveness, but some people only know anger and use it as a substitute for intimacy. Often, these people marry each other.

72. If you believe...

Comment: Equalness before the Lord and in your own mind regarding the worth of another will keep the playing field even in your relationships.

About the Author

Lynda Savage, M.S., is Director and Founder of the Center for Family Healing, a State Certified Mental Health Clinic in the State of Wisconsin. She is Founder and President of Practical Family Living, Inc., a Christian educational, not for profit agency. (pfl.org). Lynda holds a Masters Degree from the University of Wisconsin, Superior.

She also completed a two year family therapy specialist program at the Chicago Family Institute, Department of Psychiatry, Northwestern University, Evanston, Illinois. Lynda is a Clinical Member and Approved Supervisor of the American Association for Marriage and Family Therapy. Lynda has been a mental health professional for over 33 years and is a Credentialed Minister.

Additional copies of this book are available from:

The Center for Family Healing
1466 Kenwood Dr.
Menasha, WI 54952
Or dial 1-888-233-1119

This book is also available from Amazon.com or bookstores nationwide.
Ask your bookseller to order directly from Ingram,
Baker & Taylor or Bookmen.

Volume discounts are available directly from the publisher.
Visit www.savpress.com
or dial 1-800-732-3867 to place an order.